basic flavorings
Garlic

basic flavorings

Garlic

Clare Gordon-Smith

photography by

James Merrell

Whitecap Books
Vancouver/Toronto

Art Director **Jacqui Small**

Art Editor **Penny Stock**

Design Assistant **Lucy Hamilton**

Editor **Elsa Petersen-Schepelern**

Photography **James Merrell**

Food Stylist **Clare Gordon-Smith**

Stylist **Wei Tang**

Production Manager **Kate Mackillop**

Our thanks to Christine Walsh and Ian Bartlett, Mike May of Northcote Market and Mr Neo of Harrods Food Hall.

First Published in Great Britain in 1997
by Ryland Peters & Small
Cavendish House, 51-55 Mortimer Street, London W1N 7TD

This edition published by Whitecap Books Ltd.
351 Lynn Avenue, North Vancouver
British Columbia V7J 2C4

Text © Clare Gordon-Smith 1997
Design and photographs © Ryland Peters & Small 1996

Produced by Mandarin Offset
Printed and bound in China

ISBN 1 55110 563 2

Notes:
Ovens should be preheated to the specified temperature. If using a convection oven, adjust times and temperature according to manufacturer's instructions.

All pickles and preserves should be processed in a boiling water-bath canner according to USDA guidelines.

Garlic has been used as a flavoring and for its medicinal properties for thousands of years, and in many cultures. Its use was recorded in Ancient Egypt and in China as early as 2000 BC. Native to the Mediterranean and Central Asia, garlic is now used all over the world. Shown here are some of the varieties most commonly available. **Garlic chives** (left), with their flat, strappy leaves, are used as herbs. The **purple** and **white** forms of dried garlic (second from left, and center) are best at the beginning of the season; they lose flavor as the year progresses. **Elephant garlic** (second from right), has a milder flavor and is now becoming more widely available. It can be used like ordinary garlic, and is also good roasted. **Smoked garlic** (right) is becoming more widely available. Use it like dried garlic. Not shown are **fresh garlic**, available in late spring and early summer, **wild garlic**, available in spring; **garlic buds**, eaten with their stems; and **rocambole**, the mild Spanish garlic. When garlic is crushed, a complex chemical reaction takes place—an odorless amino acid, allin, combines with an enzyme allinase, which sets up a chain reaction resulting in allicin, the source of garlic's strong smell and its burning flavor.

the flavors of **Garlic**

Garlic is the basis of many great traditional flavoring combinations. Shown from left is **pesto** traditionally made with garlic, pignoli nuts, basil, and good olive oil—and also made now with ingredients such as parsley, arugula, sorrel, and even cilantro. The ubiquitous **garlic butter** (second left) is used as a

dressing on foods such as meat, poultry, fish, vegetables, escargots, and of course on garlic bread. **Aïoli** (center) is the renowned creamy garlic mayonnaise from the South of France, but its cousins are also used in Spain as *allioli* and in Greece as *skordalia*, made with the addition of breadcrumbs and pignoli nuts.

8 The flavors of garlic

Aïoli is made with olive oil, and served as a dip for crudités or young, fresh vegetables, lightly steamed and served warm. **Gremolata** (second from right), the wonderful Italian garnish made of chopped garlic, parsley, and lemon zest, is served with meat and fish. **Rouille** (far right) is the rich and unctuous mayonnaise flavored with garlic, peppers, and chiles (and here also with tomato): its name describes its color. It can be quite fiery, and is usually served with poached fish, squid, and especially with the legendary bouillabaisse, the fish soup that is almost a stew, possibly the most famous of all Mediterranean dishes.

The flavors of garlic **9**

Soups

Sweet and sour soup
with shrimp and lemon grass

Garlic is an essential flavoring ingredient in many great cuisines. In Chinese cooking, the Culinary Trinity is ginger, garlic, and scallions. It is also part of the Thai triad of flavors—garlic, ginger, and chiles.

Heat the oil in a skillet, add the shallots and garlic, and gently sauté until soft. Stir in the shrimp or scallops and gently stir-fry for a few minutes until they turn white. Pour in the white wine, tomatoes, lemon juice, fish stock, lemon grass, and kaffir lime leaf, bring to a boil and simmer for 10 minutes. Season to taste, then remove the lime leaf and stir in the cream and sliced basil. Serve, garnished with sprigs of basil and garlic croutons, if using.

1 tablespoon corn oil

2 shallots, finely chopped

2 garlic cloves, crushed

24 large uncooked shrimp, peeled and deveined, or 12 scallops

⅔ cup white wine

2 tomatoes, peeled, seeded, and diced

2 tablespoons lemon juice

⅔ cup fish stock

3 stalks of lemon grass, halved lengthwise and lightly crushed

1 kaffir lime leaf

⅔ cup cream

2 tablespoon finely sliced basil leaves

sea salt and freshly ground black pepper

to serve

sprigs of basil

garlic croutons (optional)

Serves 4

Grape harvester soup

Based on a traditional French recipe served to hungry grape-pickers. The original would have used much more garlic—perhaps as much as four heads of garlic rather than four cloves. When garlic is cooked very slowly for a long time, much of its pungency disappears—an added social benefit.

3 tablespoons olive oil

1 lb. onions, thinly sliced

4 garlic cloves, finely chopped

3 ripe plum tomatoes, peeled, seeded, and chopped

½ teaspoon sugar

5 cups vegetable stock

⅔ cup white wine

slices of stale bread

salt

Serves 6

Heat the olive oil in a saucepan, add the onions, and gently sauté until golden and very soft. Stir in the salt, garlic, tomatoes, and sugar, and cook for about 10 minutes. Add the stock and white wine, increase the heat and boil to reduce the liquid by a quarter. Simmer for about 30 minutes. Add a little extra water to thin the soup, if necessary. Place slices of bread in the base of heated soup plates, and spoon the soup over the top.

cooked slowly, for a long time, the flavor

of garlic becomes **mellow and nutty**

Spicy lentil soup
with oven-roasted garlic

Garlic is a favorite ingredient in the spicy
cuisines of India. Used with traditional
spices, it gives added zest to the earthy
and robust flavors of lentils and rice.

Cut the heads of garlic in half and place in a roasting
pan. Drizzle with olive oil and cook in a preheated
oven at 400°F for 20 to 30 minutes, or until the cloves
are soft and mushy. Set aside until ready to serve.
Meanwhile, peel and mince the ginger. Melt the
butter in a large skillet over a low heat, stir in the
ginger and spices, and cook for about 1 minute.
Add the onion, parsnips, carrot, and celery, then
season with salt and freshly ground black pepper.
Stir in the lentils and basmati rice, mixing well with
the vegetables. Add the stock and bring to a boil.
Lower the heat, cover the pot, and simmer for
about 30 minutes, until the vegetables and rice are
tender. Pour the soup into a blender or food
processor, and puree until smooth.
Return the soup to a clean saucepan, bring to a boil
and stir in the coconut milk and lime juice. Add a
little extra water if the soup is too thick.
Serve in wide soup bowls, garnished with sprigs of
basil and the roasted garlic halves.

2 small heads of garlic

olive oil, for roasting

1-inch piece
of fresh ginger

2 tablespoons butter

¼ teaspoon cayenne

¼ teaspoon allspice

¼ teaspoon cumin

a pinch of
ground coriander

1 onion, sliced

2 parsnips, minced

1 carrot, sliced

2 celery stalks, sliced

2 oz. red lentils

2 oz. basmati rice

5 cups stock

1¼ cups coconut milk

2 tablespoons lime juice

salt and pepper

sprigs of basil, to serve

Serves 4

Appetizers

Seared shrimp
with gazpacho sauce

The Spanish love garlic, and it appears in many of their most typical dishes, including gazpacho, the classic chilled summer soup based on tomatoes and garlic. It is used here in a slightly different manner, as a sauce for shrimp—another favourite Spanish ingredient.

Heat half the oil in a skillet over a moderate heat. Add 2 garlic cloves, the onion, red bell pepper, cucumber, chiles, and salt. Cook for 3 to 4 minutes. Add the tomatoes, parsley, and half the cilantro. Bring to a simmer, cover, and cook for 10 minutes. Transfer to a blender or food processor, puree, and strain into a clean saucepan. Simmer gently while you cook the shrimp, and sprinkle the remaining cilantro into the sauce. Soak wooden skewers in water for 10 minutes. Season the shrimp with salt and pepper. Thread them onto the skewers, sprinkle with the remaining crushed garlic, place under a preheated broiler, and cook for a few minutes on both sides. Serve with the sauce and a few arugula leaves.

3 tablespoons olive oil

3 garlic cloves, crushed

1 onion, sliced

1 red bell pepper, seeded and finely chopped

¼ cucumber

2 jalapeño or serrano chiles, seeded and chopped

1 lb. tomatoes, peeled and finely chopped

2 sprigs of parsley

4 tablespoons finely chopped cilantro

1 lb. large, uncooked shrimp, shelled, and deveined

salt and freshly ground black pepper

frisée or arugula leaves, to serve

Serves 4

Little red onion pies
with garlic and anchovies

Garlic and onions make a sweet filling for
these pies—serve warm with a leafy salad.

Roll out the pastry on a floured surface and use to line
four 4-inch pie pans. Trim the edges, prick with a fork,
line with foil and beans, place on a baking tray, and
cook in a preheated oven at 400°F for 10 minutes.
Remove the pie shells and reduce to 350°F. Melt the
butter in a skillet, add the onions and garlic, and
cook gently for 10 minutes. Add the wine, vinegar,
and cassis, and simmer for 30 minutes over a low
heat. Add sugar, salt, and pepper. Divide the mixture
between the pies, place 2 anchovies, if using, in a
cross on top of each, return to the oven, and heat
through for 10 minutes.

8 oz. puff pastry

2 tablespoons butter

2 medium red onions,
thinly sliced

2 garlic cloves, crushed

3 tablespoons red wine

2 tablespoons vinegar

1 tablespoon cassis

a pinch of sugar

8 anchovy fillets
(optional)

salt and freshly
ground black pepper

Serves 4

Whole baked garlic
with olives and ciabatta bread

A typical snack in the Middle East, Spain, or
Italy. Don't worry about the quantity of garlic—
roasting makes it very mellow and nutty.

Place the garlic in a roasting pan, drizzle with oil,
sprinkle with salt, and bake in a preheated oven at
400°F for 30 to 45 minutes, or until the heads are
golden brown and the cloves soft and mushy. Serve
hot with olives and toasted ciabatta.

2 whole large heads
of garlic, cut in half
crosswise

4 tablespoons olive oil

sea salt

to serve

black olives

toasted ciabatta bread

Serves 4

Wild garlic pasta
with garlic roasted butternut

1 butternut squash,
peeled, seeded,
and cubed

1 tablespoon olive oil

2–4 garlic cloves,
crushed

1 lb. fresh pasta
(made with wild
garlic if available)

sea salt

Serves 4

Wild garlic is found in springtime growing in
the fields in the English countryside. The
wonderful pungent smell of its pretty white
blossoms wafts by as you stroll through drifts
of bluebells and other wildflowers.
One of Europe's finest Italian chefs, Antonio
Carluccio, sells fresh wild garlic pasta in his
stylish Italian food shop in London's Covent
Garden. Use a similar fresh pasta if you can
find it, or substitute ordinary pasta and add
a few extra garlic cloves to the sauce. Serve
this dish with an arugula leaf salad.

Drizzle the butternut with olive oil, sprinkle with sea
salt and the crushed garlic, and cook in a preheated
oven at 400°F for about 20 minutes, or until soft.
Cook the pasta in a large pan of boiling salted water
for about 3 to 5 minutes, then drain and serve,
topped with the roasted butternut.

fresh pasta—plain

perfect team

ored with **wild garlic**—

h this **simple but unusual** sauce

Fish

Tuna burgers
with ginger and mustard glaze

Tuna flesh is dense enough to hold its texture and flavor when finely chopped with garlic and made into a hamburger patty. The ginger and teriyaki glaze becomes a sauce with a Japanese twist.

Using a food processor or a large, sharp knife, chop the tuna very finely. Transfer to a bowl and mix thoroughly with the garlic, cayenne, salt, and pepper. Divide the mixture into 4 parts, roll each into a smooth ball, then flatten into a compact patty. Chill while you make the glaze.
Combine the glaze ingredients in a large saucepan and bring to a boil. Lower the heat and simmer until the mixture just coats the back of the spoon. Strain the glaze into a pan, and reserve.
Heat the oil in a large skillet over a medium heat and sear the tuna burgers for 3 to 4 minutes on each side, until browned. Reheat the sauce.
Serve the tuna in hamburger buns, with pickled ginger slices, the reserved ginger and mustard glaze, and some Dijon mustard, if using.

1 lb. fresh tuna

2 garlic cloves, crushed

a pinch of cayenne

sea salt and freshly ground black pepper

2 tablespoons olive oil, for sautéeing

ginger and mustard glaze

4 tablespoons teriyaki sauce

1-inch piece of fresh ginger, pureed

1 teaspoon honey

1 tablespoon Dijon mustard

2 tablespoons white wine vinegar

to serve

4 hamburger buns, with seeds

1–2 tablespoons sliced Japanese pickled ginger

2 teaspoons Dijon mustard (optional)

Serves 4

Marinated tuna
with garlic white bean salad

A modern, Pacific-Rim update of that Italian classic *tonno e fagioli*, with garlic featuring in both the Japanese-style marinade and the accompanying white bean salad.

Mix the marinade ingredients together, add the tuna steaks, and place in the refrigerator for 1 to 2 hours. Mix all the salad ingredients together in a small bowl and set aside to develop the flavors. Remove the tuna from the fridge about 30 minutes before cooking. Drain the tuna and pat dry with paper towels. Pour the marinade into a saucepan, bring to a boil, and simmer until reduced to a thick sauce. Brush the fish with olive oil and place under a preheated grill for 1 to 2 minutes on each side. Top with pickled ginger and serve with the garlic-flavored white bean salad.

4 tuna steaks

2 tablespoons olive oil

1 tablespoon pickled
ginger, chopped

marinade

¾ cup teriyaki sauce

½ cup dry sherry

4 tablespoons
chopped fresh ginger

3 scallions,
finely chopped

2 garlic cloves,
thinly sliced

a pinch of cayenne

juice of 2 lemons

black pepper

white bean salad

12 oz. cooked
cannellini beans

3 garlic cloves, crushed

3 tablespoons olive oil

4 tablespoons
red wine vinegar

sea salt

Serves 4

Roasted cod steaks
with garlic tomato sauce

A deceptively simple recipe, absolutely
packed with flavor, thanks to a double
dose of garlic and tomatoes in both
the sauce and accompaniment.

Slice the tomatoes in half, top with a slice of garlic,
sprinkle with thyme, salt, and black pepper. Place in
a roasting pan, dab with olive oil, and cook in a
preheated oven at 400°F for 40 to 45 minutes.
To make the sauce, heat the oil in a skillet and gently
sauté the shallots until softened and transparent.
Add the garlic and diced tomatoes and simmer
gently for about 10 minutes.
Place a roasted tomato on top of each cod steak,
then transfer the fish to the roasting pan. Return to
the oven, dab with more olive oil if necessary, cook
for a further 8 to 10 minutes, then serve with the
garlic tomato sauce.

4 plum tomatoes

2 garlic cloves, sliced

1 tablespoon chopped
fresh thyme leaves

olive oil, for roasting

4 cod steaks

sea salt and freshly
ground black pepper

tomato sauce

1 tablespoon olive oil

2 shallots, finely sliced

2 garlic cloves, crushed

1 lb. plum tomatoes,
peeled and diced

1 teaspoon sugar

Serves 4

Red snapper
with garlic and pepper salsa

Hot pungent garlic is a flavorful addition to
this Mexican-style salsa.

4 red snapper fillets

6 tablespoons milk

2 oz. polenta grain

2 tablespoons olive oil

salsa

½ red bell pepper

½ yellow bell pepper

3 plum tomatoes

¼ cucumber

1 red chile

1 red onion, diced

2 garlic cloves, crushed

**1 tablespoon chopped
fresh cilantro leaves**

1 tablespoon lime juice

**sea salt and freshly
ground black pepper**

Serves 4

To make the salsa, core and dice the bell peppers,
peel and dice the tomatoes, peel and dice the
cucumber, and seed and chop the chile. Transfer to
a bowl and mix in the onion, garlic, cilantro, lime
juice, and seasoning.
Set aside to develop the flavors.
Dip the snapper fillets in the milk and then in the
seasoned polenta. Heat the olive oil in a skillet over
a low heat, add the fish, and cook on both sides until
lightly browned. Serve with the salsa.

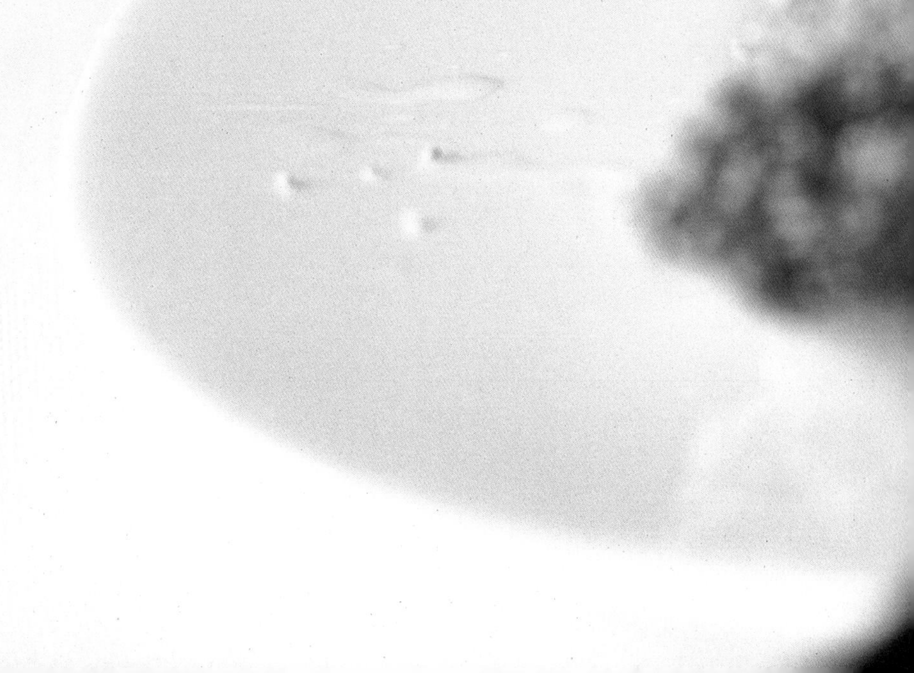

spicy garl

entree serv

Tiger shrimp
with a spiced garlic sauce

This garlic and spice mixture is an update of
an Indian original. They use garlic to flavor
the cooking oil, then sauté the spices in oil
to release the pungent aromas. It's a good
way of cooking aromatics and worth adopting
in other cooking styles too.

Heat the oil in a skillet, add the green chile, turmeric,
cumin, cayenne, tomatoes, ginger, lemon juice, and
salt, and sauté for 1 minute.
Bring to a simmer, stir in the garlic puree, add the
shrimp, cover, and continue to simmer for about
3 to 4 minutes or until the shrimp turn white. Stir in
the cilantro and serve with spiced basmati rice.

imp make a **stunning appetizer**—or an

h **spicy basmati rice** and cilantro

2–3 tablespoons corn oil

1 hot green chile,
finely chopped

a pinch of turmeric

1½ teaspoons
cumin seeds

a pinch of cayenne

1 lb. tomatoes, peeled

1-inch piece of
fresh ginger,
peeled and minced

1 tablespoon
lemon juice

1 teaspoon salt

2 tablespoons
garlic puree

1 lb. uncooked tiger
shrimp, shelled
and deveined, with
tail-fins left intact

3 oz. fresh cilantro

spiced basmati rice,
to serve

Serves 4

Meat and poultry

Sesame-coated chicken
with chile and garlic sauce

The easiest way to peel a clove of garlic is
the way the Chinese do it. Cover the clove
with the flat of a knife or Chinese cleaver and
apply a little pressure with your hand.

To prepare the pattypan squash, if using, slice off the
top, then scoop out and discard the seeds. Cook in
simmering water for 7 to 10 minutes until just tender.
Mix all the marinade ingredients together in a small
bowl. Slice the chicken into pieces, add to the bowl,
toss well to cover with the marinade, and set aside
for 2 hours or overnight.
Remove the chicken from the marinade, then toss in
the sesame seeds. Reserve the marinade.
Heat the oil in a skillet, add the chicken pieces, and
stir-fry until golden. Set aside in a warm place while
you prepare the vegetables and noodles.
Place the noodles in a large bowl, pour over boiling
water and leave for 3 minutes, or follow the package
instructions. Drain well.
To cook the vegetables, heat the corn oil in a wok,
add the zucchini and broccoli, and stir-fry for
3 to 5 minutes until cooked but still crunchy.
Place the noodles in large heated bowls, or the
cooked pattypan squash, add the stir-fried
vegetables and sesame chicken, then pour over the
reheated chile garlic marinade and serve.

1 large pattypan
squash (optional)

4 free-range
chicken breasts

3–4 tablespoons
sesame seeds

1–2 tablespoons corn oil

1 sheet of egg noodles

garlic marinade

4 tablespoon soy sauce

2 garlic cloves, crushed

1–2 red chiles, sliced

6 tablespoons sherry
or rice wine

**stir-fried
vegetables**

1 tablespoon corn oil

2 zucchini, thickly
sliced diagonally

8 oz. broccoli flowerets

freshly ground pepper

Serves 4

Chicken parcels
in a sweet bell pepper sauce

Use all red bell peppers or a mixture of red
and yellow. Peel with a potato peeler rather
than char-grilling, following French tradition
rather than the Italian. This way, their flavor
will meld more subtly with the garlic.

To make the bell pepper sauce, peel the peppers
with a vegetable peeler, cut in half, and seed.
Reserve half a red pepper and half a yellow pepper,
then slice the remainder and place in a saucepan
with the olive oil, shallots, herbs, garlic,
peppercorns, and tomato. Cook gently until soft, for
3 to 4 minutes to reduce. Add the white wine vinegar,
boil to evaporate, then reduce the heat.
Add the stock and simmer for 8 to 10 minutes.
Remove from the heat and blend for about 15 to
20 seconds to give a coarse texture. Finely dice the
reserved pepper, blanch in boiling salted water for a
couple of minutes until soft, then drain. Stir the
diced pepper and butter into the sauce.
Skin and trim the chicken breasts, then flatten them
with a rolling pin. Spread one side with olive paste,
roll up, dot with butter, and sprinkle with polenta,
breadcrumbs, and chives.
Spoon the sauce into an ovenproof dish, add the
chicken and cook in a preheated oven at 350°F for
40 minutes until golden.
Serve with a crisp green salad and crusty bread.

4 chicken breasts

2 tablespoons green
olive paste (tapenade)

2 tablespoons
unsalted butter

2 tablespoons
polenta grain

¾ cup breadcrumbs

1 tablespoon
snipped fresh chives

bell pepper sauce

2 large red bell peppers

2 yellow bell peppers

2 tablespoons olive oil

2 shallots, sliced

1 sprig of thyme

1 bay leaf

2 garlic cloves, crushed

2 teaspoons peppercorns

1 plum tomato, sliced

1 tablespoon
white wine vinegar

1 cup stock

½ teaspoon butter

Serves 4

Meat and poultry **35**

Roast chicken
with forty cloves of garlic

This is based on a traditional Provençal or Niçoise dish. It's a favorite with all lovers of great French cooking, and versions appear in many of the French culinary classics. Don't be alarmed at what appears to be a huge quantity of garlic cloves—when they are roasted whole in their skins, they develop a wonderful nutty flavor, their pungent qualities disappear, and they melt into a creamy puree. Traditionally, since the recipe originates in the South of France, it would have been slathered with olive oil—this buttery coating has been borrowed from French *haute cuisine*.

1 whole chicken, about 3 lb.

4 tablespoons unsalted butter, softened

40 whole garlic cloves, unpeeled

sea salt and freshly ground black pepper

Serves 4

Place the chicken in a roasting pan, spread the softened butter all over the skin, then sprinkle with sea salt and freshly ground black pepper. Place the garlic cloves around the chicken and cook in a preheated oven at 350°F for 1 to 1½ hours, basting regularly. To test if the chicken is done, insert a knife or skewer into the thickest part of the thigh. The bird is cooked when the juices run clear, without any trace of pink. Serve with steamed green vegetables, and boiled, minted new potatoes.

Yellow chicken curry
with coconut rice

Garlic is one of the basic flavorings in Thai cooking—part of the culinary triad of garlic, chiles, and ginger. Galangal is a cousin of ginger—if you can't find it, use ginger instead. Cilantro roots can also be hard to find. Use a bunch of the leaves instead. The flavor will be different, but comparable. Many of these ingredients are available in Asian shops and larger supermarkets.

To make the curry paste, coarsely chop the lemon grass, galangal, shallots, cilantro roots, and chiles. Place in a food processor with the remaining paste ingredients and blend until smooth. Cut the chicken into small pieces and finely chop the garlic. Heat the oil in a wok and cook the garlic until golden. Stir in the curry paste and chicken pieces. Stir in the fish sauce, stock or water, and sugar. Cut the lemon grass into 3 to 4 pieces and finely chop the lime leaves. Add the lemon grass and lime leaves to the wok, stir, lower the heat, and simmer gently for 15 to 20 minutes. If the mixture becomes too dry, add a little more stock. Meanwhile, soak the rice in cold water for 30 minutes, then place in a saucepan with the coconut milk and 3 cups water, cook for 8 to 10 minutes, then drain. Serve the curry with the coconut rice.

1 lb. chicken fillets

2 garlic cloves

3 tablespoons corn oil

3 tablespoons Thai fish sauce (nam pla)

½ cup chicken stock or water

1 teaspoon sugar

1 stalk of lemon grass

5 kaffir lime leaves

curry paste

1 stalk of lemon grass

1-inch piece of galangal or ginger

3 shallots

6 cilantro roots

4 red chiles, seeded

2 kaffir lime leaves

2 garlic cloves

1 teaspoon turmeric

coconut rice

1¾ cups jasmine rice

1 cup coconut milk

Serves 4

spicy and colorful, full of **traditional Thai** flavors—

galangal and coconut, **garlic and cilantro**

Chicken kebobs
with lime, garlic, and oregano

Serve this simple dish with harissa-flavored couscous. Harissa, the fiery North African chile-based paste, is available in gourmet shops and large supermarkets. It is easy to make yourself—just soak 1 oz. dried chiles in warm water for 1 hour. Drain and pureé with a pinch of salt, 2 tablespoons fresh cilantro, 1 tablespoon fresh mint, a garlic clove, and enough oil to make a thick paste.

Mix the lime juice with the garlic, oregano, and half the olive oil. Add chicken, and chill for 1 to 2 hours. Heat a stove-top grill-pan, add the remaining oil and sauté the onion until transparent and lightly browned. If using wooden kebob skewers, soak in water for 10 minutes. Thread the chicken strips onto the skewers and broil for a few minutes on each side. Serve, sprinkled with the oregano, together with pita bread, salad leaves, lime wedges, onion, and the spicy garlic relish.

juice of 3 limes

8 garlic cloves, crushed

1 tablespoon
dried oregano

4 tablespoons olive oil

1 lb. boneless
chicken breasts,
sliced into strips

1 onion, halved and
sliced lengthwise

2 tablespoons
chopped fresh oregano

salt and freshly
ground black pepper

to serve

pita bread

salad leaves

1 lime, cut into wedges
(optional)

spicy garlic relish
(recipe page 60)

Serves 4

Chicken breasts
with garlic butter

A modern update of the classic Chicken Kiev,
which is traditionally deep-fried.
Keeping low-fat health concerns in mind,
this oven-roasted version is much simpler.

Place the chicken breasts on a sheet of waxed paper
and place a second sheet on top. Hit the breasts with
a rolling pin to flatten them evenly.
Beat the garlic butter ingredients together then
divide the butter between the chicken breasts.
Roll up the breasts and secure with long wooden
skewers. Chill if time allows.
Mix the breadcrumbs and parsley together. Brush or
dip the chicken breasts in beaten egg, then roll in
the breadcrumb mixture. Place on a baking tray and
drizzle with olive oil. Cook in a preheated oven at
400°F for about 25 to 30 minutes until golden brown.

4 chicken breasts

¾ cup breadcrumbs
(from ciabatta olive
bread, if possible)

1 tablespoons chopped
fresh flat-leaf parsley

1 egg, beaten

olive oil, for roasting

garlic butter

4 tablespoons butter,
softened

2–3 garlic cloves,
crushed

1–2 tablespoons
chopped fresh parsley

Serves 4

Stir-fried pork fillet
with kumquat, soy, and garlic sauce

Serve this modern update of a Chinese
classic with steamed rice (basmati mixed
with wild rice is delicious) and spicy garlic
relish (page 60) mixed with chopped papaya.

Place the cornstarch, chile powder, salt, and
soy sauce in a bowl and mix well.
Add the sliced pork and leave to marinate in the
refrigerator for about 30 minutes.
Place the kumquats in a saucepan, add the sugar,
pour in about 1¼ cups water, bring to a boil, and
simmer for 15 to 20 minutes, until just tender.
Heat the olive oil and butter in a wok or skillet and,
when hot, add the scallions, garlic, and sliced pork
and stir-fry for 8 to 10 minutes until cooked through.
Add the kumquats and liquid, marmalade, and ginger.
Bring to a boil and simmer for 10 to 15 minutes.
Serve, sprinkled with fresh cilantro.

2 tablespoons
cornstarch

½ teaspoon
chile powder

a pinch of salt

1 tablespoon
light soy sauce

1 lb. pork fillets, sliced

8 oz. kumquats, sliced

4 tablespoons
raw sugar

2 tablespoons olive oil

1 tablespoon butter

1 bunch of scallions,
trimmed, and sliced
diagonally

3 garlic cloves, crushed

1 tablespoon
orange marmalade

1-inch piece of fresh
ginger, minced

fresh cilantro, to serve

Serves 4

Lamb in red wine
with potato and garlic crust

A modern update of a classic French dish—
use any cut of lamb, boned and cubed.

1 tablespoon olive oil

5 shallots, whole

2 lb. lamb, cubed

3–4 tablespoons
seasoned flour

3 whole garlic cloves

2 zucchini, sliced

6 young carrots

1¼ cups vegetable stock

⅔ cup red wine

potato crust

1 lb. new potatoes,
sliced

2 tablespoons butter

1 garlic clove, crushed

1 tablespoon chopped
fresh flat-leaf parsley

2 tablespoons chopped
fresh thyme leaves

Serves 4

Heat the olive oil in a skillet, add the shallots, and gently sauté until transparent.
Toss the lamb in the seasoned flour, add to the skillet, and sauté until browned on all sides.
Add the garlic, vegetables, stock, and wine, bring to a boil, then spoon into an ovenproof dish.
Arrange the potatoes over the top. Melt the butter in a small skillet, stir in the garlic, parsley, and thyme, and pour or brush over the potatoes. Place in a preheated oven and cook at 350°F until golden—about 45 minutes to 1 hour.

Stir-fried beef fillet
with sugar snap peas

A dish typical of Chinese and South-east Asian cooking – quick, easy and full of flavour, the very qualities that make these cuisines so popular with today's cooks. Thai fish sauce is available in gourmet shops and larger supermarkets.

Blanch the sugar snap peas in boiling water, drain, run under cold running water, then set aside until ready to serve. Cut the beef fillet into very thin slices, then set aside until ready to cook. Heat the oil in a wok or skillet, add the garlic, lemon grass, and beef slices, and stir-fry over a high heat until the meat is lightly browned. Remove the beef and set aside. Add the remaining oil into the wok, heat, then add the celery and shallots, and stir-fry for 2 minutes. Stir in the chile sauce, lime juice and leaves, fish sauce, and sugar snap peas. Serve with rice or noodles.

8 oz. sugar snap peas

12 oz. beef fillet

2–3 tablespoons corn oil

2 garlic cloves, finely chopped

1 stalk of lemon grass, finely chopped

2 celery stalks, sliced diagonally

6 shallots

1–2 tablespoons Thai chile sauce

2 tablespoons lime juice

2 kaffir lime leaves, shredded finely

Thai fish sauce, to taste

Serves 4

quick and easy, packed with Chinese and Southeast Asian **flavors**

Vegetarian dishes

Baked eggplant
and zucchini with cheese topping

Eggplant with garlic and olive oil makes a favorite Mediterranean flavor combination. This gratin-style recipe can be served as a vegetable accompaniment for meat or poultry, or as a vegetarian entree with a arugula, tomato, and basil salad.

Heat 2 tablespoons of the olive oil in a medium skillet over a low heat. Add the onion and cook for about 15 to 20 minutes, stirring occasionally, until tender and golden. Add the eggplant, cook for about 3 to 4 minutes, then add the zucchini and garlic, and sauté until tender. Sprinkle with salt and allow to cool.

Beat the eggs with the remaining olive oil, balsamic vinegar, cream, and Parmesan, then sprinkle with pepper. Stir in the sautéed vegetables. Spoon the vegetable mixture into an ovenproof baking dish 9 inches square, and cover with foil. Cook in a preheated oven at 325°F for 35 to 40 minutes, until just set. Remove the foil, sprinkle with the remaining Parmesan, and broil until golden. Serve with an arugula, tomato, and basil salad.

3 tablespoons olive oil

1 onion, thinly sliced

1 medium eggplant, sliced and diced

8 oz. green zucchini, sliced

8 oz. yellow zucchini, sliced

2 garlic cloves, finely chopped

2 eggs

3 tablespoons balsamic vinegar

1 cup heavy cream

¼ cup shredded Parmesan cheese, plus 2 tablespoons, for topping

salt and freshly ground black pepper

salad, to serve

Serves 4

Garlic ratatouille
baked in butternut shells

Ratatouille is one of the greatest of all
vegetable dishes—and tastes best when each
kind of vegetable is cooked separately first,
then put together and cooked further.
Ratatouille can also appear as a dish in its
own right when served in this unusual way—
as a filling for sweet butternuts. This makes
a popular vegetarian dish served with a crisp
salad, such as Belgian endive.

1 butternut squash

1 tablespoon butter

4 tablespoons olive oil

2 onions, chopped

4 garlic cloves, crushed

1 eggplant, cut
into 1-inch cubes

2 zucchini,
cut into ¾-inch slices

4 plum tomatoes,
seeded and quartered

1 red bell pepper,
seeded and diced

1 yellow bell pepper,
seeded and diced

sprigs of fresh
marjoram and thyme

½ cup breadcrumbs

sea salt and freshly
ground black pepper

Serves 4

Cut the butternut in half, scoop out and discard the
seeds, brush the cut sides with butter, and cook in a
preheated oven at 400°F for about 15 minutes.
Heat 3 tablespoons of the olive oil in a skillet. Add
the onions and garlic, and gently sauté for about
5 minutes, until soft. Add the eggplant and sauté
until just golden. Remove from the skillet. Add the
tomatoes and peppers, and cook until tender, adding
a little more oil when necessary.
Return the eggplant and onions to the skillet, and
stir in the herbs and seasoning.
Spoon the mixture into the butternut shells, sprinkle
with breadcrumbs, cook at the same temperature for
20 minutes, then serve.

Vegetable pilau

Pilaus and their pilaf cousins are found all over South and Central Asia, in the Middle East, the Mediterranean, and everywhere that Moghul or Moorish influence is found. The method is similar to risotto, where flavorings such as garlic, onions, or spices are first cooked in butter or oil, then the rice is stirred in, followed by boiling stock. Rinsing the rice first removes some of the starch, so the grains remain separate.

flavor

Place the rice in a bowl and wash in several changes of water, until the water runs clear. Drain, cover with water, leave to soak for 30 minutes, then drain and leave in a strainer for 20 minutes.

Cut the potatoes into chunks, trim the carrots and slice in half, trim the beans and cut into pieces.

Heat the oil in a heavy skillet, then add the cumin seeds and let them sizzle for 5 to 6 seconds. Stir in the carrots, potatoes, and green beans and sauté for 1 minute. Stir in the drained rice, salt, and remaining spices, together with the chile, cilantro, ginger and garlic. Sauté for 2 to 3 minutes. Add 2½ cups water, bring to a boil, cover tightly, reduce the heat to low, and cook for 25 minutes. Remove from the heat and let stand for another 10 minutes.

Serve, sprinkled with sprigs of cilantro.

glorious and **golden yellow,** a classic dish
h **garlic and spices**

1½ cups basmati rice

4 oz. potatoes

8 oz. baby carrots

2 oz. green beans

1 tablespoon corn oil

1 teaspoon
whole cumin seeds

a pinch of salt

½ teaspoon turmeric

1 teaspoon ground
cumin seeds

1 teaspoon
ground coriander

¼ teaspoon cayenne

½ green chile, seeded
and finely chopped

2 tablespoons finely
chopped fresh cilantro

1-inch piece of fresh
ginger, minced

2 garlic cloves, crushed

2½ cups water

sprigs of cilantro,
to serve

Serves 4

Vegetables **55**

Vegetable sofrito
with chile sauce and tortillas

Sofrito sauces are typical of Spanish and
Italian cooking. In Spain, annatto seeds are a
typical ingredient, while in Italy it's made
with garlic, onions, celery, peppers, and
herbs, and sometimes with tomatoes, as it is
here. The sauce is used to flavor all kinds of
dishes, including soups and entrees. This
version has a South American influence,
served with tortillas and hot chile sauce.

Heat 2 tablespoons of the oil in a large skillet, then
add the onions, bell pepper, and garlic and cook
gently for about 10 to 15 minutes until soft.
Stir in the tomatoes and sherry, season to taste, then
simmer for about 30 minutes.
Melt the butter in another skillet and gently sauté the
pumpkin for about 5 to 7 minutes until golden brown,
then remove from the skillet, stir into the sofrito, and
simmer for about 15 to 20 minutes.
Heat the remaining oil in the skillet, add the okra,
and stir-fry gently for a few minutes, then add to the
sofrito mixture. Serve with steamed rice, tortillas,
and a dash of hot chile sauce.

3 tablespoons corn oil

2 onions, chopped

1 red bell pepper,
seeded and
finely chopped

4 garlic cloves, sliced

15 oz. canned chopped
tomatoes, or
1 lb. plum tomatoes,
peeled and seeded

4 tablespoons sherry

2 tablespoons butter

1 lb. pumpkin, peeled,
seeded, and cut into
large chunks

8 oz. okra, trimmed

to serve

8 oz. cooked rice, such
as a mixture of white
long-grain and wild rice

flour tortillas

hot chile sauce

Serves 4

Homemade pizza
with garlic roasted zucchini

What would pizza be without garlic! Roast
the garlic and vegetable topping first for a
sun-roasted Mediterranean flavor.

2 tablespoons olive oil

4 yellow zucchini,
sliced

3 garlic cloves, sliced

4 tablespoons chopped
fresh thyme leaves

sea salt

pizza dough

1 tablespoon
fresh yeast

¾–1 cup milk

2 cups all-purpose flour

a pinch of salt

a pinch of sugar

2 tablespoons olive oil

Serves 4

To make the pizza dough, cream the yeast in a bowl
with a little milk. Place the flour in a bowl with the
salt, sugar, olive oil, creamed yeast, and just enough
milk to form a stiff dough.
Using the palms of your hands, knead on a floured
surface to form a smooth dough.
Return to the bowl, cover with a clean kitchen towel,
and leave to rise in a warm place for about
30 to 40 minutes until well risen.
To make the topping, heat the olive oil in a skillet,
add the zucchini and garlic, and sauté gently for
a few minutes.
Knock back the dough and knead for a few minutes,
then roll out on a floured surface, to fit a greased,
8 x 10-inch baking pan.
Place the dough in the pan, and pull it into the
corners. Top with the sautéed vegetables, sprinkle
with thyme, and cook in a preheated oven at 400°F
for about 20 minutes, or until risen and golden.
Serve, cut into pieces.

Spicy garlic relish

To get the best and brightest flavor, add the
garlic at the last minute.

Squeeze the lemon. Chop the parsley and garlic.
Peel, seed, and chop the tomatoes. Roast, skin,
seed, and finely chop the pepper. Heat the oil in a
skillet, add the tomatoes, and sauté for a few minutes.
Spoon into a bowl, then add the cumin, harissa,
4 tablespoons of lemon juice, and 3 tablespoons
parsley. Mix well, then add the garlic, mix again,
then taste and season.

1 lemon

4 tablespoons chopped
fresh flat-leaf parsley

4 garlic cloves

6 plum tomatoes

1 red bell pepper

2 tablespoons olive oil

1 teaspoon cumin seeds

1 tablespoon harissa
paste (see page 41)

salt and pepper

Serves 4

Garlic cilantro sauce

A wonderful dressing to pour on avocado
salad, or as a dip for crudités.

Place all the ingredients in a bowl and mix well. Chill
for a few hours until ready to serve.

⅔ cup sour cream

3 tablespoons chopped
fresh cilantro

1½ tablespoons
chopped fresh parsley

1 teaspoon finely
chopped red onion

2 garlic cloves, crushed

grated zest and
juice of 1 lime

2 teaspoons honey

Serves 4

Pickled tomatoes

**Vary the chile quantity according to taste—
the red serranos are sweeter than the green.**

Place the garlic in a food processor and puree with a little olive oil. Cut the tomatoes in halves or quarters, and place in a clean jar. Slice the scallions and chiles and add to the tomatoes. Pour the vinegar into a pan, bring to a boil, add sugar and salt, then stir for 1 minute until dissolved. Remove from the heat. Heat the oil in a skillet, add the pureed garlic and the spices, and cook for about 2 minutes until the aromas are released. Remove from the heat and stir in the vinegar. Pour into the jars, cool, seal, and refrigerate until ready to use. Keeps 1 month.

8 garlic cloves

1 cup olive oil

1 lb. plum tomatoes

1 bunch of scallions

4 serrano chiles (red and green), seeded

scant 1 cup vinegar

½ cup brown sugar

1 tablespoon sea salt

2 tablespoons olive oil

1 tablespoon black and yellow mustard seeds

1 teaspoon peppercorns

Makes 4 cups

Tomato rouille

Blanch the garlic, pepper, and chiles in a pan of boiling water for 3 to 4 minutes. Remove with a slotted spoon and reserve. Place the egg yolks in a food processor and blend for 2 to 3 minutes until thick. Add the garlic, red pepper, chile, and ketchup, and blend until smooth. With the motor running, pour in the oil in a a slow steady stream until the sauce resembles a thick cream. Season, then serve.

8 garlic cloves

1 bell pepper, seeded

2 red chiles, seeded

2 egg yolks

2 teaspoons tomato ketchup

1¼ cups olive oil

salt and pepper

Makes 2 cups

Above, from left, Spicy garlic relish
(recipe page 60), Tomato rouille,
and Pickled tomatoes (page 61).

Index